HARLEY-DAVIDSON
CUSTOMS

Tim Remus

Motorbooks International
Publishers & Wholesalers ®

First published in 1995 by Motorbooks International Publishers & Wholesalers, PO Box 2, 729 Prospect Avenue, Osceola, WI 54020 USA

Motorbooks International books are also available at discounts in bulk quantity for industrial or sales-promotional use. For details write to Special Sales Manager at the Publisher's address

Library of Congress Cataloging-in-Publication Data Available

ISBN 0-87938-989-3

On front cover: It's hard to resist the allure of Arlen Ness' old chopper theme, especially when it's done up with a great set of overlapping flames applied to a specially shaped gas tank and Taildragger rear fender.

On the frontispiece: Wayne Benson's FXR sports sexy Viper billet wheels and brake calipers from Performance Machine. The swingarm is a dual-rail model from Arlen Ness.

On the title page: Brad Cullen's Softail shows just enough chrome and polish to look good in contrast with the wild paint job. The engine is a business-like mixture of S&S crank and pistons for total displacement of 96 cubic inches.

On the back cover: Charlie Anderson raked his FXR's frame an extra three degrees and then lowered the bike four inches at both ends. The rest of the equipment is a mix of one-off parts, like the unique swingarm, combined with Arlen Ness and Custom Chrome bits.

Printed and bound in Hong Kong

Contents

Acknowledgments

This book contains more than thirty bikes, which means there are far too many to thank each owner or builder by name. There are, just the same, a few individuals who need to be singled out. Steve Laugtug, for example, must be thanked for allowing me access to his elaborate photo studio. And my lovely and talented wife Mary must be thanked for rinsing all that film in the Motel room sink after the Pepsi can exploded in the cooler. Yes, the same cooler that contained all the film I shot in Daytona.

To all the rest, I have to offer a collective thanks—for showing up on time, for moving the bikes a million times, for filling out the technical sheets, and mostly for being patient.

Russ Tom created a unique ride by combining a FXR chassis with a FLH front end, complete with the big front fender and headlight nacelle.

Introduction

The Harley-Davidson world, and custom Harley-Davidsons in particular, is moving pretty fast these days. What were cutting edge bikes only four or five years ago are now quite common. Every time I go to Sturgis the bikes aren't just better, they're a lot better than they were one year before. The design, the execution, the paint and assembly—all the things required to build a great bike have improved dramatically in the past few years.

There are new people coming into the sport (the ones that some old timers grouse about), and they bring with them new ideas and sophisticated fabrication skills. More riders and enthusiasts means that there's a larger pool of talent and money to draw on. Money attracts parts manufacturers, so there are more parts in the catalogs than ever before. And those parts aren't just widgets or skull-shaped valve caps for your tires. There are some pretty slick new calipers and wheels carved from large chunks, or billets, of aluminum on computerized lathes and mills. Arlen and Cory Ness have introduced a whole line of billet parts, everything from handlebar grips to lifter blocks. And a host of formerly automotive-only companies are hot on their heels with new designs.

New sheet metal designs are turning up, too. Now there are more than two gas tanks in the catalog, presumably because the market is big enough to warrant the tooling required to knock out new shapes. And covering all that sheet metal on the newest bikes is some outrageous paint. The colors offered by House of Kolor and PPG, among others, are nothing short of electric. The new urethane paints are super vibrant, very durable and easier to spray (though they still require caution in their use due to the toxicity of the chemicals). The new paints and increasing skills of the custom painters mean that the new bikes carry brighter reds and softer pearls than ever before.

The Harley-Davidsons in this book represent some of the best of the new breed of customs. Broken down by model "family," I've tried to include both the high-dollar bikes that garner all the press, as well as the less expensive machines built by individuals in home shops. Though the book doesn't detail all the features on the bikes, the captions are as informative as I could make them in order to answer the many questions you'll surely have about each motorcycle.

My own bias runs toward designs that are simple (though there's at least one very gaudy Harley-Davidson included here). I prefer bikes that rely on the strength of the design, rather than the number of widgets or murals, for their good looks. I also feel that custom bikes should be functional with good handling and brakes. The bikes presented here, though varied, reflect my opinions and tend toward the simple and sanitary.

These are good-looking bikes. As much as possible, they represent a cross-section of the custom bikes from Main Street America. I hope to have captured not only the bikes but a little of the energy that the bikes represent. If the book had a soundtrack, it would be the rumble of multiple V-twins running hard down the main drag of Sturgis or Daytona. Can you hear it? Good. Now crank the volume, and open the book.

1 Sportsters

Not Necessarily Basic

A good design has a certain staying power, witness the old VW "bug," the Chevy small-block V-8, and, of course, the Harley-Davidson Sportster. First introduced in 1957 (though the K models were available earlier without the Sportster moniker), the Sportster was and is a great-looking bike. There's nothing extra here, just an engine, a gas tank, and two wheels. As delivered, these are basic motorcycles, well built and well proportioned. Rare is the Sportster that remains basic for very long, however.

In days of yore, the Sportster was the bike to have. The over-forty crowd will remember the magic letters "XLCH." They held a certain allure for any kid with a little gasoline in

Simple and tasty, Jim and Jeannie Shaller's Sportster started life as a stock, 1993, 883. With the addition of a few body pieces, a nice paint job, and some accessories, this "little Harley" is transformed into a striking motorcycle. Grips and mirrors are from the Kuryakyn catalog as is the air cleaner, which gives the Sportster the look of a larger bike with a killer motor.

The unique gas tank is a factory CR item. This is actually the second tank. The first was mounted solid to the bike and developed cracks due to vibration. Underneath all the shine is a 74-cubic-inch Ironhead engine with a stroker bottom end, ported heads, S&S carburetor, and fabricated exhaust based on a set of XLCR pipes.

his veins because the hot rod Sportster was said to be the fastest bike on the street. When the chopper phenomena hit in the late 1960s, Sportsters remained tremendously popular. Bike shows of the period were filled with Sportsters modified with hardtail kits and long, springer front forks.

Eventually the Big Twin replaced the Sportster as the bike to have. Hot rodders say it's hard to beat cubic inches, and the Big Twin offered more cubes and more potential for raw horsepower. Big Twins became more "macho" than Sportsters and more likely to be modified and customized. Sportsters became the bike to ride rather than the bike to customize.

But there have always been die-hard Sportster supporters among the ranks of Harley-Davidson owners—men and women who will ride nothing else, and who sell one Sportster just to buy another. In the past, anyone who wanted to customize a Sportster had to rely on hand-fabricated or adapted parts, as the number of aftermarket parts designed for the Sportster was relatively small.

That situation has changed recently, and the major aftermarket companies like Custom Chrome, Drag Specialties, and Nempco all offer tanks, fenders, wheels, and a variety of accessories built strictly for the Sportster line. You can make a Sportster look like a Big Twin or a cafe racer with parts right out of the catalog. Or you can mix and match and create your own version of the ideal Sportster.

Bob Heinze used a 1977 Sportster as a starting point for creating a personalized Sportster CR. By combining a factory CR gas tank with a cafe style fairing and minimal rear fender, Bob created a unique Sportster with the look of a CR. While the factory CR used black on black for a sinister look, Bob's cafe racer uses red flames over burgundy base paint, combined with plenty of chrome and polish for a very bright package.

Left, this bike is a combination of off-the-shelf parts and hand-fabricated hardware. The front fairing and fender are from Arlen Ness, and the gas tank is from Harley-Davidson. Unique oil tank, fender struts, and exhaust were built by Donnie Smith. Cast wheels are from Harley-Davidson and painted to match the bike.

Bill Messenbrink's Sportster is based on a 1977 frame stretched two inches to accept an XLCR gas tank. The cafe fairing, longer tank, scalloped paint job, and sleek profile make the bike look trim and fast. The Sportster taillight is molded into what was an FL front fender and mounted to the bike with modified FX fender struts. Under the fender sits a 150x16-inch tire, which requires off-set sprockets so the chain will clear the tire.

In the past couple of years, buying a new Harley meant knowing your dealer, paying a premium, or waiting patiently for your name to come up on a long list. The most popular of the hyper-popular Harleys are the Big Twin models. This means that recent buyers often get a Sportster simply because they can have one today instead of waiting until three years from next Tuesday. These new buyers then take advantage of the parts in the catalogs to create a bike of their own.

Savvy buyers understand that the Sportster to have is the smaller 883 model. It's a lot cheaper than the 1200, and it can be bumped to the larger capacity with relative ease. With the additional displacement and a few key parts, a 1200 Sportster will put out more than seventy horsepower at the rear wheel—enough to turn the "little Harley-Davidson" into a true hot rod that will stomp most of its bigger brothers.

The bikes shown here represent both ends of the spectrum. The Ironheads are built with stretched frames and plenty of hand-fabricated parts while the other bike is a more modern Evolution model built

14

The front spoiler doubles as a small oil tank and was fabricated by Messenbrink. Not only does it add capacity to the system, it also acts as a radiator to keep the engine cool. An Arlen Ness cafe fairing helps give the bike its go-fast look. Lower fork legs are chrome plated as are the Harley-Davidson calipers. The unusual front fender is a Sportster unit turned end-for-end and modified with extra skirting.

Left, Bill Messenbrink's old
Ironhead engine uses an S&S bottom end and 0.030-over pistons for a displacement of 74 cubic inches. An older S&S Series-B carb feeds gas and air to ported heads with valves operated by four Sifton minus-minus camshafts. Each cylinder head is tapped for an extra spark plug, which are fired by Dyna coils and a Dyna single-fire ignition. Chrome-plated fins on the heads and cylinders shine brightly.

with aftermarket parts. Like all good customized motorcycles, paint plays a key part in all four designs. The bikes looks are very different from one another and help to illustrate the point that a good builder need not be limited by the basic nature of a Sportster. Though they start out kind of short and basic, they certainly don't have to stay that way.

At nearly forty years of age, the Sportster shows no gray hairs and seems, in fact, to be the eternal adolescent. Never overweight and never out of style, the Sportster remains a wonderful motorcycle and a good starting point for a personalized Harley-Davidson.

Left, all that glitters is not chrome. In this case the glitter comes from powder-coated rocker boxes, engine cases, and exhaust pipes combined with a flat black Dell'Orto carburetor and cylinders.

Above, Orville built himself a very tasty Ironhead Sportster with some unusual wheels, a solo seat, cafe fairing, and a nice black with gold leaf paint job.

2 The FXR Models

Born to Boogie

O riginally known as Super Glide II, the FXR series Harley-Davidsons were introduced late in 1981. Though the lines at first seem similar to those of the earlier FX Super Glide, the FXR was a whole new motorcycle.

The frame, for example, was computer designed to be five times stiffer than the old FX frame. Instead of bolting the engine directly into the frame, it was (and still is) supported by a three-point suspension system (known on the street as "rubber mounted"). Instead of a four-speed, the new bike came with a five-speed trans-

The nice orange paint job by Jerry Scherer, the extra fork rake, and lowered stance give Donnie Smith's FXR a nice, clean look. Note the molded frame, paneled area under the seat, and use of paint instead of chrome for many of the parts and accessories. Ported heads—shaved for more compression—work in conjunction with the Andrews EV3 cam, Series-E carburetor, and Arlen Ness/SuperTrapp exhaust pipe to produce good, usable horsepower for the street.

Like the frame, the sheet metal on this bike consists of modified Harley-Davidson components. The taillight is molded into the FXR fender, and the gas tank is missing the console, instead using a small "Donnie Smith special" gas cap. Brake calipers are from GMA, and the wheels are polished and painted Harley-Davidson items.

mission. Though the first bikes were equipped with the Shovelhead engine, by 1984 all FXR Harley-Davidsons were equipped with the Evolution engine.

The engineers designed the new frame with the battery and oil tank tucked neatly under the seat. Thus these bikes seem much more streamlined than the older bikes. The wheelbase on the FXR, at 64.7 inches is just more than 2 inches longer than the 62.3 inch wheelbase of the early Super Glides. The combination of a longer frame and tucked in oil tank and battery give the FXR a smoother look than the older FX.

Well-known bike builder Dave Perewitz has commented that when you strip an FXR they get long and low—and that seems to be the way most customized FXRs turn out. Though you can build an FXR into any kind of bike you want, the long, lean look seems to prevail. When Arlen Ness bolted a small cafe fairing to the front of a slammed FXR he started another styling trend that continues to this day. To say the catalogs are filled with parts for the FXR is an understatement. A mountain of aftermarket fenders, side covers (from Arlen again), seats, and exhausts prove that this is a very popular bike in customizing circles.

With the rubber-mounted engine, a stiff frame, and good suspension, the FXR is a bike that lends itself to a certain hot rod theme. An FXR can be hopped up, customized, and even lowered (as long as the owner doesn't go too far) and remain a ridable, comfortable bike that handles well. With an FXR, a prudent customizer

Wayne wanted a radical but ridable bike. Jim Thompson of Cylinder Head Service installed all new bottom end components but retained the stock stroke. The heads were reworked with a good port job, new, larger valves, and higher-quality springs and keepers. Wayne did the final assembly himself, using a Redshift 575 cam, chrome moly pushrods, and an S&S "shorty" carburetor.

Wayne Benson's FXR benefits from a much-modified frame—the rear section has been widened and the front section is brand new. Note that the flattened fender rails are part of the frame. With all that custom frame work, stock sheet metal just wouldn't cut it. The gas tank started life as a police tank, then was stretched ten inches at the back and shaped to wrap around the front of the Danny Gray seat. To fill the new, wider rear frame section, the stock FXR fender was widened nearly two inches. In front, an aftermarket fender was grafted to a FXR fender bracket. When all the fabrication was finished, the frame and all the sheet metal were molded and finished by Don Perewitz of Cycle Fab fame.

can have his cake and eat it too by building a good-looking bike with all the right stuff—one that can still be ridden on a daily basis. In fact, one of the bikes seen here—the orange FXR— is the daily rider for well-known customizer Donnie Smith.

Though the bike remains very popular, the FXR models have been phased out by Harley-Davidson to be replaced by the new Dyna Glide line. Men and women on the street don't seem to care that the model is on its way out. They're still building FXR bikes with everything from modified stock V-twins to full-on stroker motors with nitrous oxide. Forks are kicked out with extra rake to create what Donnie Smith calls, "A bike with an attitude." With shorter fork tubes or spring kits for the front forks and shorter rear shocks, the height comes down (more easily than

Tom from Carlton Harley-Davidson in Mantua, Ohio, massaged Andy's Evo with ported heads, an Andrews EV3 camshaft, and a Series E S&S carburetor. A good motor should show as well as go, so Andy used chrome rocker covers, primary cover, coil cover, an S&S air cleaner to contrast with the otherwise Lumina-red V-twin.

Andy Drobnjakovic's FXR features Harley-Davidson forks lowered with a set of White Bros. fork springs. The solid front wheel is from Rev Tech and measures 21 inches in diameter. The front fender and cafe-style fairing are both from the Arlen Ness catalog.

with a Softail by the way), and then it's a matter of choosing the right sheet metal and a sufficiently brilliant paint job.

If there's a trend of late, it's toward longer bikes with custom sheet metal and beautiful, bright paint. The FXR again lends itself to the long look. Some builders can't get enough of a good thing and build FXRs with stretched frames and stretched gas tanks to match. Arlen Ness has capitalized on this concept with his Luxury Liners, which seem to me more like a Dresser than a hot rod FXR (see the Dresser chapter for one example of a very long, low FXR).

The bikes shown in this chapter run the gamut from relatively simple machines to elaborate projects that took many months and many dollars to complete. Some have been lowered, painted, and souped up. Others ride on modified frames with extra rake, equipped with hand-crafted sheet metal and completely polished and chrome-plated engines. Wayne's red FXR is one such bike, built

Drobnjakovic calls this FXR his first "serious" Harley-Davidson. The molded frame and mostly stock sheet metal wear red paint in a Chevy Lumina shade. Some not-so-stock sheet metal is seen at the rear, where the cat's eye taillight is frenched neatly into the rear fender.

Next page upper left, Dan figures he's got 3,500 hours invested in the fabrication of flames, not including final polishing and plating. Dan cut each flame from sheet steel, heated it with a torch to shape it, and then sanded the edges.

Next page lower left, the outside of Dan's V-twin has been treated to two-tone powder coating and engraved and chrome plated covers. Inside there are Wiseco pistons, ported heads, a Crane cam, and a Series-E carburetor from S&S.

Drag bars with speedo and tach mounted beneath and a Softail-style rear fender give Ray Puglisi's FXR a sleek look all its own. The paint is white pearl from House of Kolor with hot pink and purple graphics. Note the carb hanging off the wrong side.

Previous page right, Dan Sudnick's FXR features flames in the paint and flames in 3-D. The front fender is from an FLH, narrowed to fit the FXR narrow-glide fork. The rear fender is from an FXR and modified to resemble the front. Juan Villicana from The Fantasy Studio sprayed the wild paint job which took five weeks to complete.

Next page left, Puglisi's FXR uses Rev Tech Wheels and GMA brake hardware mounted to a stock frame. The front fender is from the Arlen Ness catalog; the front and rear of the bike have been lowered two inches.

Next page right, Ray's chrome plated V-twin retains the stock 80-cubic-inch displacement, but that's about all. High compression pistons, ported heads, Crane cam, and a unique intake with two Dell'Orto carbs make this V-twin look and run like nothing else.

Charlie's FXR dates to 1982 and thus uses the Shovelhead for power. This example uses a Sifton #102 camshaft and a S&S Series-E carburetor to improve breathing and performance.

around an FXR frame with a new front frame section, a modified rear section, some very classy sheet metal, and first-class wheels and hardware.

Big, hot rod engines call for fat rear tires, which don't fit easily between the arms of a stock swingarm. This then requires a conversion from the factory belt, to chain drive. That's all fine and good as long as the drive sprocket lines up with the driven sprocket—and the fender is wide enough to cover the new tire. One seemingly small change often begets another and another until very little of the original bike remains.

Variety is the spice of life, as shown by the FXRs in this chapter. Some were built by professionals, and others were bolted together by "amateurs" using all their skill (and probably all their money). No matter, they're all lovely and they're all functional. In the best FXR tradition, these are all hot rod Harleys, and they're all "riders."

3 Softails

Never Stock for Long

Designed to look like a true "hardtail," the Harley-Davidson Softail uses a triangulated swingarm and hides the spring/shock units under the transmission. Considered by many to be Harley-Davidson's single best marketing move in the past ten years, the introduction of the Softail gave Harley-Davidson sales a jump-start and created a lot of work for customizing shops as well. Introduced as an extension of the then-current Wide Glide, the addition of Fat Bob tanks, a long Wide Glide fork, and a variety of accessories made the Softail a factory-built custom.

Al Verduzco's Fat Boy wears a great pearl paint job and just enough accessories to set it apart from the crowd. Al's mostly stock Evo breathes through a Kuryakyn air cleaner and expels spent gases through a two-into-one exhaust. A variety of small things help set off this Fat Boy from the crowd, like the drag bars with billet grips, the nice forward controls, and the chrome cover for the rear frame section.

The unusual paint job on the Fat Bob tanks was created by first painting the bike black, then taping off the scallops and spraying them with a splatter gun. The custom dash is an item from the Arlen Ness catalog.

Left, note the extensive use of paint even on things like the headlight housing—a part that would normally be chromed or polished.

Above, Tank Ewsichek's bright Softail rolls on Performance Machine wheels—a 16-inch front and an 18-inch rear. The front fender is from a Heritage, and the rear fender—supported by Custom Chrome fender rails—was created by joining two Heritage fenders.

Bob Lowe's softail is truly an original, made up mostly of hand-formed panels and parts. Wheels are aluminum hoops from Custom Chrome, brake calipers are from The Motor Company.

The V-twin carries high-compression pistons and a Crane cam. Gas and air are mixed in the S&S carb, fired by a Dyna single-fire ignition, and exit via the custom two-into-one exhaust.

Ron Englert formed the unique gas tank from scratch, working sheet steel on an English wheel. FLH-style headlight nacelle has been blended with the bars and the tachometer housing to form a very slick assembly. Note the flush-mount gas cap.

Though it may not look it, this nifty swingarm started life at The Motor Company. Eccentric axle adjusters are the handiwork of Roger Bergei of A.C. Customs. Fabricated taillight housings double as fender struts and look as though they might have come from a 1953 Buick.

Though all Harleys seem destined for modification and customizing by their owners, the Softail seems like the ideal bike for men and women who want to build a motorcycle unlike any other parked at the curb. With an engine solidly bolted into the frame and limited suspension movement, the Softail might not be the road bike an FXR is, but when a bike looks this good who cares about suspension travel?

At the time of its introduction there were only two Softail models. Today the Softail frame is the basis for a at least four separate families of motorcycles. The pop-

Ed Kerr's softail is unlike any other. The more you look, the more you see. The oil tank has "tails" welded on so it better fills the area below the seat. Nifty air cleaner is the work of Ken Rasp and was fabricated from sheet aluminum. The rear of the Softail frame has been cleaned up and modified to neatly accept the fabricated rear fender struts. Between the fender struts is a modified Arlen Ness Taildragger fender with a flush-mount taillight.

The Arlen Ness front fender wraps around a 21-inch spoked rim supported by a Springer fork assembly. Performance Machine four-piston calipers slow it all down.

Left, the floorboards are hand crafted—including the rubber strips—as were the small panels between the primary cover and the frame. The good-looking V-twin features polished cases and cylinders with polished fins (in fact, the lower fins were polished right off the cylinders) all painted red to match the bike.

Wild paint and first class components make for a modern, sophisticated Softail. Mike Ethier's bike uses a stock frame, aftermarket fenders, and modified 5-gallon Fat Bob Tanks. Note the flush-mount taillight and frenched license plate. A low stance was achieved by using White Bros. springs in the front fork and a modified swingarm with Fournales shocks in back.

Left, though the engine displaces only 80 cubic inches, it cranks out 80 horsepower at the rear wheel as measured by the Custom Chrome dynamometer. Power is achieved through the use of modified heads, high lift camshaft, S&S Super G carb, Bartels pipes, and Dyna 2000 single-fire ignition.

Above, derby and inspection covers, as well as the mirrors, are part of the Mirage accessories set from Custom Chrome. Transmission is a stock five-speed with belt-drive to the rear wheel. Billet wheels as well as four-piston brake calipers are from Performance Machine.

ularity of the machine, and the tendency of Softail owners to personalize their bikes, means that the catalogs from the major aftermarket companies are filled with Softail accessories.

Softails lend themselves to a variety of styling themes. The rigid-look frame means they're a natural for any kind of old-time or nostalgic theme. Mix an early-style oil filter, horn, and tool box with the

Everybody wants their bikes long and low. Brad Cullen's yellow Softail was lengthened by mating an Arlen Ness front section to a Harley-Davidson Softail rear frame section. Additional fork rake and low stance enhance the effect of

the stretched frame. To fit the longer frame, the Fat Bob tanks have been lengthened 3-1/2 inches and wrap neatly around the seat. Instead of a conventional dash and gauges, Brad chose a neat "no gauges" dash for the clean look.

Left side shows more of what makes the nostalgia theme work: chrome sprocket cover, tombstone taillight, white grips—to match the white leather seat and pillion—and fringed, white leather lever covers.

right paint job, and the bike suddenly appears much older. Or add a genuinely old fork assembly, as one of our owners did, and the bike looks as though it was built before the war.

If FXR models lend themselves to the long, lean look, Softails lend themselves to the fat profile. Equipped with fat, tail-dragger fenders, Fat Bob tanks, and sixteen-inch wheels on both ends, the bikes are anything but skinny. Maybe this trend is fueled by the aging motorcycle riding population. It seems that as the average age of the riders goes up (and often the weight as well), so does the size and weight of their motorcycles.

Because the shock/spring units are hidden, the bikes take on a completely different look than a FXR or Dyna Glide. Though these bikes are a natural for a chopper look, the lack of visible rear suspension components also make them candidates for

Right, sunfire yellow and linen cream white paint, a chrome tool box, fishtail pipes, and early-style horn all reinforce the old-time theme.

The engine on Mike's ride is nearly stock. The air cleaner is from Drag Specialties. Note the horn, tank logo, oil filter, and the louvered dash panel between the tanks.

Left, Don Hotop doesn't believe in using a lot of off-the-shelf accessories. Thus we see a one-off air cleaner with an interesting milled pattern—a pattern repeated on the ignition and transmission covers and the plug for the oil tank.

Above, there isn't much here that isn't essential to the operation of the motorcycle. The frame is molded with integral fender rails, and the gas tank features a small, custom dash with speedometer. The air dam is a Hotop trademark. Wheels are from Harley-Davidson, polished and painted for extra allure. GMA provided the brake calipers, though the milled pattern is Hotop's own.

an ultra-modern, sophisticated look. Without any shock absorbers in the way, a builder or designer can pay more attention to the sheet metal at the bike's rear. To see just how far you can go with the design of a very slick motorcycle, just check out Bob Lowe's black Softail in this chapter.

Though some riders and builders prefer FXRs and some like a Dresser, there are

probably more customized Softails than any other single model. The bikes in this chapter include the already mentioned future-bike look, along with more traditional custom bikes. There are also Fat Boys (but no Fat Girls) with tremendous visual impact, though in truth they remain

If you look closely, you'll see a small 4-Valve logo on the rocker covers that identify this as a V-twin with Fueling Stage III four-valve head kit. The kit includes the four-valve heads two S&S carburetors, and Fueling exhaust.

close to stock. And then there are Softails that retain very little of their original frame or sheet metal. In between are a number of what can only be called, "Main Street Customs," or bikes you might admire as they sit outside a local bar or restaurant.

Ron Rupp's sleek Springer gets its attitude from the extra fork rake and the lower-than-stock height. Ron used visual tricks to lower the bike further, including a lowered front fender and headlight and a lowered rear fender mounted with Arlen Ness fender rails.

Left, the flamed paint job wasn't enough; note the flamed Corbin seat and flamed Arlen Ness billet grips. The 21-inch spoked front rim is combined with an 18-inch Performance Machine rear rim and a 140-series Metzeler tire.

These machines are definitely different from the FXR bikes, and they're different from each other. Some are fat, and some are relatively thin. Some carry the sixteen-inch front wheel close to the frame while others kick a twenty-one-inch spoked rim way out in front. Most use all of the Harley-Davidson frame, though at least one uses an aftermarket frame. One bike uses a "Softail" frame fabricated from 4130 Chrome Moly steel in conjunction with a swingarm that includes an integral brake caliper cut from two pieces of billet aluminum. Perhaps better suited to the Customs chapter, this particular bike uses modified upside-down forks and sheet

The primary drive consists of a special drive pulley with a spring-loaded compensator, a Gates Poly-Chain belt, and a fabricated clutch basket. Little John's idea was to eliminate anything that wasn't essential and to shrink the parts that were. Note the "forward controls" coming off the carved-from-billet primary cover.

Previous page, a "Softail" in design only, Gary Newton's bike was fabricated by Little John Buttera. The frame is 4130 Chrome Moly, and the swingarm—with integral brake caliper—was carved from aluminum billet. The fork is a White Power upside-down unit. Steve Davis crafted the tank, fenders, and oil tank from sheet steel or aluminum.

Right, the gas tank is made up of smaller sheets of aluminum shaped on a power hammer and then welded together. Air is drawn through a hand-hammered air cleaner, mixed with gas by an S&S Super-G carburetor, then fed to ported Harley-Davidson heads. Even the exhaust system was carefully formed by hand to have just the right shape.

Springer fork and early fender create much of the old look for this modern bike. Both Wheels are 16-inch Harley-Davidson items with rechromed rims and stainless spokes. Note the light bar, Deluxe logo, and nifty front fender light.

Right, Alan Webber's Hardtail isn't really a Hardtail, though it isn't really a Softail either. The hybrid design uses a Softail-type frame from Tripoli Inc. and a 1946 springer fork assembly, complemented by sheet metal and accessories possessing that old-time look.

Next page left, Evo engine gives it away—this ain't really an old Hardtail. Engine is stock except for S&S shorty carb and an early-style air cleaner. Transmission is equipped with Andrews components for a lower first gear and the mandatory kick start lever. Cat-eye dash and Fat Bob tanks look right at home.

Denis' Plante's softail custom bike uses 16-inch rubber on both front and rear. Drag-style handlebars are from a Canadian company called Slight Mod and wear Arlen Ness grips and mirrors. A stock Harley-Davidson rear wheel was modified to fit the front, then chrome plated. The fork is longer than stock and features polished and machined lower legs.

Previous page right, Denis' V-twin retains it's 80-cubic-inch displacement, though it breathes through ported heads with the help of an S&S cam and carburetor and a pair of Bartels' Performance pipes. The unusual white-blue-flamed paint job was designed and applied by the owner.

Plante's Softail Custom turned into a true custom Softail with the addition of a great paint job, a longer front end, new fenders, Corbin seat, and Arlen Ness taillight.

metal fabricated by one of California's most talented "tin men."

These bikes offer a window into the collective imagination of America's gearheads and motorcycle enthusiasts. Before you decry the lack of skill or imagination shown by today's workers, look again at these motorcycles. The old-world skills, the imagination, the willingness to take risks, those seemingly lost abilities are alive and well—in the world of customized Harley-Davidsons.

4 Dressers

Traveling in Style

The first Dresser was born—rather than created—when some rider mounted leather bags and a canvas windshield on some very early model Harley-Davidson. Always close to their riders, the factory first sold these items as part of their own line of accessories and eventually offered the bikes equipped with bags and windshield, or "already dressed" if you will. Personalizing those early bikes was usually done by adding more of the same—more lights, crash guards, and bumpers for the fenders.

Always a solid part of the Harley-Davidson landscape, Dressers were, until recently, seen as "adult" motorcycles.

Left side of Tank's dresser shows it to be the most modern of rides. Note the monochromatic paint job, frenched taillight, coral paint job, and extended fenders. Rear view shows off the cat's eye taillight set into the fender and the total lack of chrome. The bike has been lowered 2 inches at both ends, and extended fenders make it seem lower than it really is.

Lenny and Connie Schwartz started with a very rough 1975 FLH then applied their sign painting (and mechanical) skills to transform it into this very contemporary cruiser. Note the whitewall tires on spoked rims, paint instead of chrome on many parts, and the modern graphics.

Fiberglass bags were widened and the rear fender features a frenched license plate and taillight. Pinstripes and graphics are Lenny's own.

What the kids would call an old man's bike—big, slow, and comfortable like an old Buick. No one could stretch their imagination far enough to see the potential inherent in these big motorcycles.

The old Shovelhead engine has been rebuilt and now carries an Andrews H-grind camshaft for more power. Air cleaner and battery box are painted in pearl white to match the rest of the bike.

Adrian Newkirk started his project with a stretched, raked FXR frame, and then added a 39mm Wide Glide fork mounted in Arlen Ness billet triple trees. The dual-rail swingarm is from Arlen, too, as are the Taildragger fenders. The gas tank was stretched to match the longer frame.

All that has changed.

In recent years there are more and more Dressers on the streets, and more and more of them are being customized. Instead of adding widgets and accessories, the new breed of owner is removing things from the motorcycle. Donnie Smith and Drag Specialties were on the leading edge of this trend with the wonderful red and silver Dresser they introduced a few years ago.

Lowered, painted, and stripped of some bulk, the new Dressers are good looking bikes, with the essence of the design left intact and fewer distracting

The front fairing is a much-modified FXRT unit with hand-formed "lowers." Dual disc front brakes use Performance Machine calipers mounted to powder-coated lower legs. This long, radical ride rolls on Metzeler 18-inch tires mounted to spoked rims.

What separates Adrian's bike from similar machines are the details. Things like the hand-formed trim at the edges of the fenders and the taillight and license plate set into the rear fender.

lights and bezels to distract the viewer. Once again close to its customers, Harley-Davidson is cashing in on this trend with the new Road King (put your name on a list now for delivery some time in the next century) and before that the FLH Sport. FXRTs (a Dresser in my book) have suddenly reached Most Popular status and qualify as a good starting point for a wild customizing job, as evidenced by the work of both Arlen Ness and Donnie Smith. Older Shovelhead FLH bikes have become classic icons like some kind of two-wheeled '59 Cadillac.

Maybe it's the baby boomers getting older and going slower with more comfort. Whatever the reason, the big bikes are suddenly very, very popular and ripe for a variety of modifications. FXRTs can be stretched and slimmed to create a cruise missile for the highway—with a radar detector as standard equipment. FL series bikes need only to be slammed, painted, and trimmed of some windshield height to qualify as hot cruising material for cool riders. With the right "old" parts, Dressers can become nostalgia bikes, much like certain Softails. Stripped of all but the most essential gear and painted in a wild 1990s paint scheme, the bikes are as modern and zoomy as a stretched-out FXR.

The aftermarket companies have made it easier for riders to customize their big bikes with a series of new parts designed especially for them. The new catalogs list shorty windshields, lowering kits, FLH-style

Right, the engine in Doug's ride is an Evo left mostly stock excepting ported heads, a Crane Cam, and an S&S carburetor. Note the speedo housing integrated into the gas tank and the graphics by Roy Mason and Nancy Brooks.Chapter 5

headlight nacelles, and dual exhaust systems all designed for "Hogs." What was an old man's bike or the one reserved for long trips has become a neat way to get around on two wheels. Men and women who ride Dressers no longer need to apologize because their bike isn't a Softail or an FXR.

The bikes presented here are but the tip of the iceberg, the first wave of what is sure to be a brace of newly customized Dressers. The first bike is one of those FXRT highway bikes. A Dresser that's definitely not an FLH but is equally cool nonetheless. Two of the bikes are Shovelhead FLH bikes, but you couldn't find two similar bikes that look more different. One uses classic styling cues and a modern paint job for a look that's both traditional and unique, the other uses one-off sheet metal to create a new-wave design reminiscent of certain automobiles of the 1950s.

Consider these bikes an appetizer tray designed to whet your appetite for the full course of Dressers to follow in the next few years.

Next page, Doug's late-model FLT got the smooth and modern treatment with help from Cycle Fab. Note the FLH headlight nacelle, the mostly monochromatic paint job, and the additional fork rake.

5-Customs

In a Class by Themselves

There's no doubt, Harley-Davidson builds good-looking motorcycles. With certain modifications and paint, the factory bikes can be made to look even better—or at least less like the other Softails or FXRs on the street. Yet, there are certain limitations imposed by the parts themselves. No matter how much you modify an FXR, it's still an FXR. At some point, it becomes easier and less expensive to start from scratch rather than spend a tremendous amount of time and money modifying an existing motorcycle.

Much of the unique sheet metal on Wink Eller's bike is shaped from aluminum sheet, including the side panels, rear fender/seat pan, and the chain guard. The gas tank is a Sportster unit. This 80-cubic-inch Evo is designed to run in the open-wheeled, stock displacement class at both El Mirage and Bonneville. By running with and without nitrous, one bike can compete in two classes. Engine cases are from House of Horsepower, and the heads were ported by Jerry Branch. Carburetor is a Super G from S&S, and the exhaust is Wink's own.

For individuals who insist on only the best, or those who want to start their project with a clean piece of paper, there is the full custom motorcycle. Pick a frame from Arlen Ness or Tripoli or Drag Specialties or Custom Chrome. Now, go out and buy a motor at a swap meet or over the counter at your local dealer (not always easy to do) or have one built from aftermarket components. You need a transmission too, and will the primary drive be a chain or belt? How about the drive to the rear wheel?

Next, select the tank(s), fenders, wheels, and all the rest of the items on your list. Now, mock everything up in your shop, modify and alter certain parts to fit like they're supposed to, and then pull everything apart again for painting and plating. Finally, you get to assemble and ride your "new" motorcycle.

It ain't easy, and it certainly isn't cheap, but it does allow the builder a tremendous amount of freedom—freedom to put together a bike with exactly the characteristics and design he or she wants. Long and lean or short and fat, Softail or Hardtail, springer or hydraulic fork, what you want is what you get. Usually reserved for serious Harley fanatics and professional bike builders, the custom route is becoming more and more popular.

As the price of new Harley-Davidsons continues to rise, it becomes easier to justify the expense of building a bike from scratch. Expanded aftermarket offerings also make it more alluring to build this way by offering the potential builder a

Metzeler rear tire measures a wide 170/55x18 inches and connects by chain to a modified five-speed gear box.

larger parts bin to chose from.

Most of the bikes seen in this chapter were built by professionals like Donnie Smith or Dave Perewitz. They represent the pinnacle of custom bike design and assembly. These are full-on, "take no prisoners" custom motorcycles. If what the bike needs is a longer tank, then someone makes one. If the radius of the fender doesn't match the radius of the wheel, well someone modifies the fender until it does—or they make a fender from scratch.

Wink Eller used a Paughco Hardtail frame, FXR forks, some very nice hand-formed panels, and a NOS-equipped motor to create this wild red Bonneville bike. Spoked Akront rims measure 18 inches on both ends and Performance Machine calipers slow everything down.

The machines shown include blower bikes; long, stretched-out creations; short and stubby scoots; and a few Hardtails. Like I said earlier, with a true custom bike, you can have anything you want. Exotic or functional, it's all possible and it's probably represented here.

There's no skimping on parts. The hardware on these bikes is all top shelf. Most roll on wheels made from an aluminum rim mated to spokes cut from billet 6061 T6 aluminum. Brake calipers, too, have been cut from billet aluminum on computerized

The special Cycle Fab fabricated swingarm makes it possible to run a fat, 180x17-inch Metzeler tire and retain the belt drive. The FXR fender was widened to cover the new tire and modified to accept the flush-mount taillight. Wide tire and belt drive combination meant Dave spent a lot of time during the mock-up stage positioning the engine, transmission, and rear wheel.

Left, Mike Brown's very long orange custom is based on an Arlen Ness five-speed frame, a stroker motor, and some very special sheet metal. The front fender is a modified Sportster unit, the rear fender came from an FXR, and the gas tanks started life as 3-1/2-gallon Fat Bobs. The air dam is a "Hotop Special."

Unusual wheels and six piston calipers are the latest in high performance machinery from Performance Machine.

CNC equipment before being polished or chrome plated. The plumbing between the caliper and master cylinder is high-quality, braided stainless steel line.

Before these bikes are painted, the frames

Left, Not just any old Evo, this is an 89-cubic-inch stroker built from polished Delkron cases and an S&S bottom end, topped with painted and plated Harley-Davidson barrels and heads—all fed by a new Mikuni 42mm flat-slide carburetor.

The fenders are Taildraggers from Arlen Ness, while the oil tank, primary cover, and chain guard have all been fabricated by Mal Ross. The idea was to keep this Shovelhead skinny, hence you see fender struts that wrap around slender fenders, the tapered FXR tank, Narrow Glide fork, and sectioned handlebars.

and sheet metal parts are "molded" or smoothed out with filler so that all the seams and welds disappear, and the elaborate paint jobs go on a perfectly smooth surface.

The paint jobs themselves involve a number of steps. First the primer is applied, then the base coat followed by pearl or candy colors, and then the clear coat. Graphics are applied after the final color, unless the builder is after a special effect like ghost scallops (which are applied someplace in the middle of the candy coats). The finished paint job lies flat and perfect, without a flaw or ripple on an absolutely smooth surface. The perfection exhibited in these bikes—exemplified by the paint jobs—isn't an accident, it comes from careful planning, thorough

This 80-cubic-inch Shovelhead was completely rebuilt before being installed in the frame. Inside is an S&S bottom end, Wiseco pistons, and Andrews camshaft. Outside, it's brandywine paint combined with polished cam and rocker covers.

Right, this Mal Ross custom is based on a hardtail frame, Shovelhead engine, and some unusual body work. Note how the pipes run uphill at the same angle as the bars and how the air cleaner's shape mimics that of the gas tank.

To achieve a different look, Dave Perewitz used a wide-glide front end. Performance Machine supplied the 17x3-inch spun-aluminum front wheel which is mated to an Avon tire. Four-piston calipers are from PM as well.

Left, Dave's front fender is from a Fat Boy while the rear is a widened FLH unit modified to accept the flush-mount taillight. The rear fender was widened to straddle the 160x17-inch tire mounted to the Performance Machine aluminum rim.

Perewtiz's long purple Harley-Davidson gets its people-pleasing power from the Arlen Ness five-speed frame, wide-glide fork, one-off tank, and great magenta paint applied by the team of Perewitz and Perewitz.

Below, this Evo is a little unusual in that it breathes through an SU carburetor and ignites with a Morris magneto. Under all that chrome and glitter is a stroker motor with a 4-5/8-inch bottom end and 3-1/2-inch pistons from S&S. The guts are harbored in Delkron cases and topped by Harley-Davidson cylinders and heads.

The engine in Larry's sanitary ride is a balanced and blueprinted 80-cubic-inch Evo with Crane Cam, S&S Series-E carburetor, and Bub pipes. The powder-coated white engine wears limited chrome and dove-tails nicely with the motorcycle's overall design.

Right, Larry Page wanted a simple motorcycle, so he chose a Pro Street frame without extra stretch or rake (and no side covers), combined with an uncluttered 80-cubic-inch engine, simple sheet metal, and a clean paint job. Front and rear billet wheels are the new Viper design from Performance Machine. PM was chosen to supply the four-piston calipers as well.

Previous page right, the gas tank started as a Super Glide tank, though it's hard to recognize. Mr. Giggie at Departure Bike Works installed a flush-mount gas cap and stretched the tank 3 inches to better fit the frame.

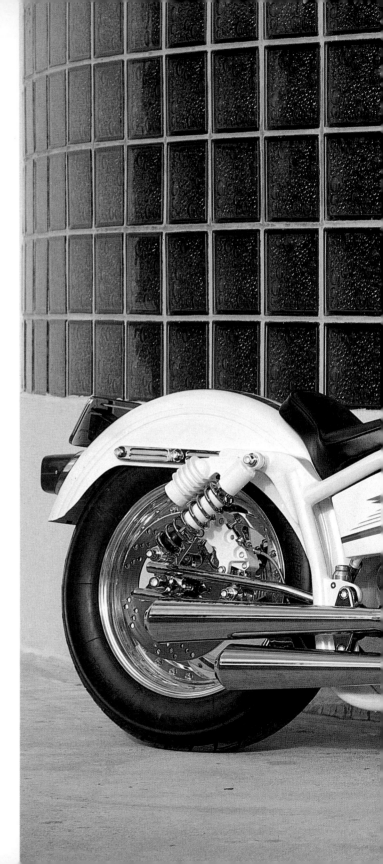

The old Shovelhead engine powers this chopper, but it's been rebuilt and equipped with some of the very latest in accessories—like a billet air cleaner and flamed points cover. Cases are polished, while the barrels and heads were chrome plated then painted red to match the bike.

Left, a true chopper needs all the right stuff, and this Arlen Ness special has it—a pre-Evo V-twin, a Hardtail frame with a short springer front end, a 21-inch spoked rim, no front fender, and ape-hanger handlebars. Arlen likes to mix the old with the new, thus we have a billet chain guard and grips, flamed derby cover, and new-wave floorboards.

Delkron cases form the foundation for this 80-cubic-inch mill. Cylinders and ported heads are from The Motor Company. The V-twin inhales through a Model B S&S carburetor with help from an S&S 561 camshaft and exhales into a pair of Bub pipes. A Primo belt drive carries power to the transmission. Note the one-off belt cover.

Right, the Five-Bs Pro Street bike is based on a stretched Tripoli hardtail frame, an 80-cubic-inch Evo engine, shortened Harley-Davidson fork tubes, and a stretched gas tank. Note the milled recesses on the calipers and brackets.

The same, only different. The Donnie Smith-built bike in the foreground mounts the blower on the right, uses flames sprayed over near-stock sheet metal, and a small fairing for a wild but conventional look. Steve Laugtug's bike however mounts the blower on the left and uses pastel colors and modern graphics sprayed over modified sheet metal for a very 1990s appearance.

preparation, and painstaking attention to detail during the application.

The finished machines are larger than life, often built by professionals for special customers or simply to highlight the shop's abilities—an expensive rolling billboard if you like. Elaborate and beautiful but functional as well, these bikes do run. In fact they roar with the bellow of modified V-twins built with that same "take no prisoners" attitude used on the rest of the bike.

A feast for the eyes and ears, these bikes provide inspiration for all the riders who haven't gotten that far yet. As a long, orange creation roars down main street Daytona, a hundred heads turn and at least half of those heads wish and promise that "some day, I'm going to have one of those."

Index